Best Easy Day Hikes
Raleigh-Durham

Help Us Keep This Guide Up to Date

Every effort has been made by the authors and editors to make this guide as accurate and useful as possible. However, many things can change after a guide is published—trails are rerouted, regulations change, facilities come under new management, etc.

We would love to hear from you concerning your experiences with this guide and how you feel it could be improved and kept up to date. While we may not be able to respond to all comments and suggestions, we'll take them to heart and we'll also make certain to share them with the authors. Please send your comments and suggestions to the following address:

> The Globe Pequot Press
> Reader Response/Editorial Department
> P.O. Box 480
> Guilford, CT 06437

Or you may e-mail us at:

> editorial@GlobePequot.com

Thanks for your input, and happy trails!

Best Easy Day Hikes Series

Best Easy Day Hikes
Raleigh-Durham

Peter Reylek and Lauren Reylek

FALCONGUIDES

GUILFORD, CONNECTICUT
HELENA, MONTANA

AN IMPRINT OF THE GLOBE PEQUOT PRESS

FALCONGUIDES®

Topo! Explorer software and SuperQuad source map courtesy of
National Geographic Maps. For information about TOPO! Explorer,
TOPO!, and Nat Geo Maps products, go to www.topo.com or www
.natgeomaps.com.

Maps by Offroute © Morris Book Publishing, LLC

Library of Congress Cataloging-in-Publication Data

Reylek, Peter.
  Best easy day hikes, Raleigh-Durham / Peter and Lauren Reylek.
    p. cm. – (Falconguides)
  ISBN 978-0-7627-5439-7
1. Hiking–North Carolina–Raleigh Metropolitan Area–Guidebooks.
2. Hiking–North Carolina–Durham Metropolitan Area–Guidebooks.
3. Trails–North Carolina–Raleigh Metropolitan Area–Guidebooks. 4.
Trails–North Carolina–Durham Metropolitan Area–Guidebooks. I. Reylek, Lauren. II. Title.

  GV199.42.N662R356 2009
  917.56'55–dc22
                                                    2009018890
Printed in the United States of America

10 9 8 7 6 5 4 3 2 1

Contents

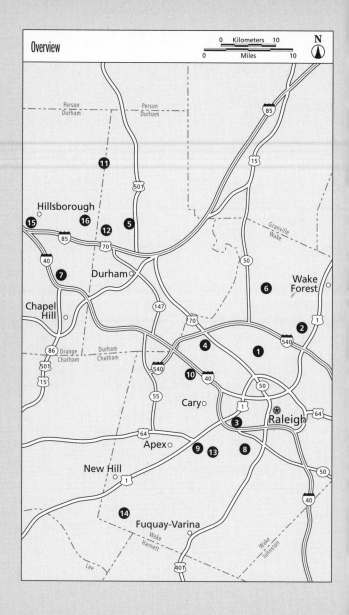

Kilometers

Miles

N

Person
Durham

Person
Durham

11

501

Hillsborough

15

16

12

5

85

70

40

7

Durham

147

Granville
Wake

50

6

Wake
Forest

2

1

70

70

540

1

Chapel
Hill

86

Orange
Chatham

Durham
Chatham

540

10

40

4

1

55

50

501

15

Cary

1

64

3

Raleigh

64

Apex

9

13

8

New Hill

1

50

14

40

Fuquay-Varina

Wake
Harnett

Wake
Johnston

Lee

401

Acknowledgments

The authors would like to thank their friends and family for their love and support. Thanks also to our editor, Scott Adams, for his guidance.

This book is dedicated to the memory of Linda Peabody Reylek, whose love of learning and the written word will always be a source of inspiration.

Introduction

The Raleigh-Durham area is a rare treasure for day hikers. Both cities have a wealth of lakes, rivers, parks, greenways, and natural areas. From here you are literally within minutes of dozens of hiking opportunities, and there always seems to be a new hike to discover.

For this guide we've chosen sixteen of our favorite local hikes. Each is convenient to the Raleigh-Durham area and can be hiked in a few hours at most. You'll find a representative variety of what the region has to offer, with riverside strolls, historical sites, wheelchair-accessible nature paths, family outings, and secluded getaways.

We've included optional extended hikes for many of these trips to help you begin to branch out and explore. We think these are sixteen parks that you will want to visit time and again. Many adventures await you in North Carolina.

Weather

North Carolina's mild climate allows for comfortable hiking virtually year-round. Warmer winter days can be a great time to hike, when the insects are dormant and the woods are clear and open.

The state's natural beauty is at its best in temperate spring and autumn months. Wildflowers are abundant in the spring, and in the fall the changing foliage is worth a special trip.

Summers in central North Carolina can get very hot. Temperatures in excess of 90 or even 100 degrees are common. Sunscreen, a wide-brimmed hat, and an extra water supply are essentials for summer hiking. In recent years drought conditions have been common, so do not depend on backcountry water sources without confirming current local conditions.

Restrictions and Regulations

The following governmental and nonprofit organizations manage the public lands described in this guide, and can provide further information on these hikes and other trails in their service areas.

- North Carolina State Parks, NC Division of Parks and Recreation, 1615 MSC, Raleigh 27699-1615; (919) 733-4181; www.ncparks.gov; parkinfo@ncmail.net. A complete listing of state parks is available on the Web site, along with park information, brochures, and maps.

- City of Durham, Parks and Recreation Department, 101 City Hall Plaza, Durham 27701; (919) 560-4355; www.durhamnc.gov; Rhonda.Parker@durhamnc.gov. A complete listing of Durham parks is available on the Web site, along with park information.

- City of Raleigh, Parks and Recreation Department, 2401 Wade Avenue, Raleigh 27607; (919) 831-6640; www.raleighnc.gov; PRContact@ci.raleigh.nc.us. A complete listing of Raleigh parks is available on the Web site, along with park information, brochures, and maps.

- Town of Cary, Parks, Recreation, and Cultural Resources Department, 316 North Academy Street, Cary 27513; (919) 469-4061; www.townofcary.org; mary.henderson@townofcary.org. A complete listing of Cary parks is available on the Web site, along with park information. Some brochures and maps are available.

- Wake County Parks, Recreation, and Open Space Department, WC Parks, P.O. Box 550, Suite 1000, Raleigh, NC 27602; (919) 856-2667; www.wakegov .com. A complete listing of Wake County parks is available on the Web site, along with park information, brochures, and maps.

- Orange County Parks and Recreation Department, Central Recreation Center, 300 West Tryon Street, P.O. Box 8181 Hillsborough, NC 27278; (919) 245-2660; www.co.orange.nc.us. A complete listing of Orange County parks is available on the Web site, along with some park information.

- Triangle Land Conservancy, 1101 Haynes Street, Raleigh 27604; (919) 833-3662; www.triangleland.org; info@tlc-nc.org. A complete listing of TLC parks is available on the Web site, along with park information, brochures, and maps.

Park regulations regarding trail use may vary. Please obey all local regulations and be considerate of the parks and other visitors.

Safety and Preparation

The hikes listed in this guide are local, popular, and relatively safe. However, a small problem on the trail can quickly become magnified if help is not readily available. Make sure you are prepared for an emergency even on short hikes.

- Carry a daypack with essential gear (listed in the next section).
- Pack a small first-aid kit on even the shortest hike. Know how to use it. Be prepared to treat minor injuries such as bug or animal bites, stings, cuts, fractures, or sprains.
- Familiarize yourself with the trail map before your hike. Let someone know where you'll be, and when possible, hike with a partner or group.
- Be prepared for changing weather conditions. Check the forecast before heading out. Bring rain gear if necessary. Wear extra layers in the cold that you can remove if you get too warm. Use sun protection, including a hat, in the heat.
- In any weather, bring a full water bottle, and an extra water supply for longer hikes. Dehydration can quickly become a serious problem, even a short distance from help. Stop and rest as much as necessary.
- Don't drink from untreated water sources (lakes, streams, etc.). Chemical treatment or a filter is needed to protect from microbial contamination.
- Do not touch or feed wildlife. Even cute animals such as rabbits may bite, and they may carry disease.
- Bring a cell phone (with the ringer off) in case of emergency. Be aware, however, that not all parks will have full cell coverage.

Day Hiking Checklist

There are a few essential items a day hiker should bring along on even the shortest trips. These basics will help you find your way, protect you from the elements, and can be easily assembled in a small day pack.

- Extra water
- Extra food
- First-aid kit
- Compass and map (a GPS is a good supplement, but carry a compass as a backup)
- Sun protection (sunscreen, hat, sunglasses)
- Insect repellent
- Fire-starting gear
- Flashlight
- Pocketknife
- Emergency whistle
- Extra clothing

Zero Impact

The trails in this area are popular and often heavily used. As trail users and advocates, we must be especially vigilant to make sure our passage leaves no lasting mark. Here are some basic guidelines for preserving trails in the region:

- Pack out your own trash, including biodegradable items like orange peels. You might also pack out trash left by less considerate hikers.
- Don't approach or feed any wild creatures—the squirrel eyeing your snack food is best able to survive if it remains self-reliant.
- Don't pick wildflowers or gather rocks, antlers, feathers, or other treasures along the trail. Removing these

items is prohibited in all parks, and will only take away from the next hiker's experience.

- Avoid damaging trailside soils and plants by remaining on the established route. This is also a good rule of thumb for avoiding poison ivy and other common trailside irritants.

- Preserve plants and wildlife by keeping your pets on a leash at all times. Unleashed dogs are prohibited at all parks for their safety and the safety of other visitors.

- Don't cut switchbacks, which can promote erosion.

- Loud noises can disturb wildlife as well as other hikers. Be courteous by not making loud noises while hiking.

- Many of these trails are multiuse, which means you'll share them with other hikers, trail runners, mountain bikers, and equestrians. Familiarize yourself with the proper trail etiquette, yielding the trail when appropriate.

- Use bathroom facilities at trailheads or along the trail.

How to Use This Book

This guide is designed to be simple and easy to use. Each
chapter includes a map and summary information that deliv-
ers the trail's vital statistics including length, difficulty, fees
and permits, park hours, canine compatibility, and trail contacts. Directions to the trailhead are provided, along with
a general description of what you'll see along the way. A
detailed route finder (Miles and Directions) sets forth mile-
ages between significant landmarks along the trail.

Hike Selection

The hikes in this guide are all found within an easy drive of
Raleigh or Durham, generally less than 30 minutes. They
range in difficulty from quick strolls under a mile to rugged
6-mile treks.

There are sixteen of the area's best hikes, but this list is
by no means definitive. With so many local hikes to choose
from, and so many individual preferences, each hiker will
have his or her particular favorites.

There is much more to explore in the Raleigh-Durham
area, and even in these specific parks, than can be encompassed
in one short guide. By the time you've completed all sixteen
recommended hikes, you should have a great handle on the
area, and be ready to branch out and explore new places.

Difficulty Ratings

The hikes in this book are arranged in order of difficulty,
beginning with the easiest.

These are all easy hikes, but easy is a relative term. To aid in the selection of a hike that suits particular needs and abilities, each is rated easy, moderate, or more challenging. Bear in mind that even the most challenging routes can be made easy by hiking within your limits and taking rests when you need them.

- **Easy** hikes are generally short and flat, and should be suited to even the most inexperienced hikers.
- **Moderate** hikes involve rougher trails and mild changes in elevation, and may take longer to complete.
- **More challenging** hikes feature some steep stretches and will take the longest, per mile, to complete.

These are completely subjective ratings—consider that what you think is easy is entirely dependent on your level of fitness and the adequacy of your gear (primarily shoes). Factor in the trail length when planning your hike. If you are hiking with a group, you should select a hike with a rating and distance that's appropriate for the least fit and prepared in your party.

Approximate hiking times are based on the assumption that on flat ground, most walkers average 2 miles per hour. Adjust that rate by the steepness of the terrain and your level of fitness, and you have a ballpark hiking duration. Of course, be sure to add more time if you plan to picnic or take part in other activities like bird-watching or photography.

Trail Finder

Best Hikes for Backpackers

Best Hikes for Great Views

Best Hikes for Nature Lovers

Best Hikes for Lake Lovers

Map Legend

85	Interstate Highway
70	U.S. Highway
55	State Highway
2003	Local Roads
= = = = = = =	4WD Roads
-----------	Featured Trail
- - - - - -	Trail
~~	River/Creek
⬭	Bodies of Water
- - - - - -	County Boundary
▭	Park Boundary
‖‖‖‖‖	Boardwalk
⏝	Bridge
✪	Capital
🏫	Park Office
P	Parking
🐾	Picnic Area
■	Point of Interest/Structure
🚻	Restroom
○	Town
11	Trailhead
🔭	Viewpoint/Overlook
❓	Visitor/Information Center

1 Shelley Lake–Sertoma Park

This paved loop trail is a wonderful way to enjoy nature without venturing too far from civilization. The loop takes you on a stroll around 53-acre Shelley Lake, a nesting area for hawks, herons, geese, and ducks. Distance markers and workout stations along the path make this a perfect place to go for exercise. The park offers excellent wheelchair/stroller accessibility and amenities to make a great family trip.

Distance: 2.8-mile loop

Approximate hiking time: 1–2 hours

Difficulty: Easy due to mostly wide, paved trails

Trail surface: A paved trail around lake and an unpaved forested trail

Best season: Spring

Other trail users: Mountain bikers, joggers, dog walkers

Canine compatibility: Leashed dogs permitted

Fees and permits: No fees or permits required

Schedule: Dawn to dusk

Water availability: Concession stand

Maps: USGS Raleigh West, NC; trail map available inside the Sertoma Arts Center

Jurisdiction: City of Raleigh Parks and Recreation Department

Trail contacts: Shelley Lake, 1400 West Millbrook Road, Raleigh 27614; (919) 420-2331; www.raleighnc.gov

Finding the trailhead: From U.S. Highway 70, turn onto West Millbrook Road. Travel 2.8 miles and on your left you will see a Shelley Lake sign; turn left onto Gardencrest Circle, which leads into the park. The trailhead is to the left of the Sertoma Arts Center. *DeLorme: North Carolina Atlas & Gazetteer*: Page 40 B2. GPS Coordinates: 35° 51' 32.0" N / 78° 39' 54.2" W

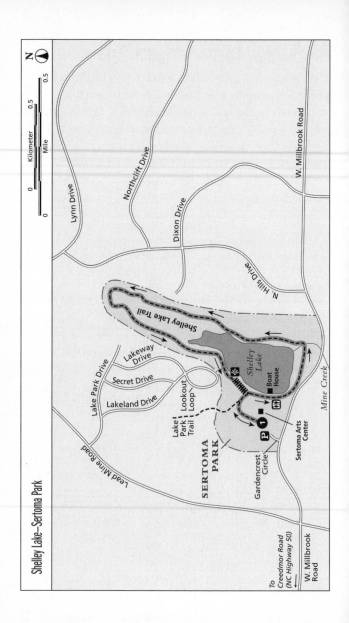

Shelley Lake–Sertoma Park

The Hike

This city park is a great place for hikers of all skill levels. The park offers amenities including the Sertoma Arts Center, free fishing rod rentals, playgrounds, fields, exercise stations along the paved loop trail, and a concession stand.

Although swimming is not permitted, fishing is encouraged. Largemouth bass, sunfish, bream, and catfish are a few of the species you can catch as you watch herons fishing on the opposite bank.

Begin this hike by heading downhill from the parking lot toward the lake. You'll pass the arts center and playground on your right. The trails are wide and paved, but be prepared for some hills.

The loop trail begins at the lake. At the fork there is a large boardwalk. Head right on the loop and you'll begin a short uphill climb to the top of the earthen dam. As you walk along the dam, you'll have a great view of the lake. This is a good place to spot hawks and herons.

Distance markers in half-mile increments are posted along the trail, helpful if you want to measure your pace. Various exercise stations are also situated alongside the trail if you're inclined to add a few sit-ups or pull-ups to your hike.

At several points the Shelley Lake Trail connects to the Raleigh Greenway system. Bear left at the intersections to continue hiking around the lake.

You'll see a changing topography as you make your way around the tapering north end of the lake. Be on the lookout for woodpeckers where the woods are thickest.

As you return to the boardwalk you'll have a final viewing opportunity from the wooden observation platform.

As you head back uphill from the boardwalk, the Lake Park Trail branches off on your right. Unlike the park's other trails, Lake Park Trail is not paved, instead taking you on a wooded stroll along the creek. The 0.3-mile spur crosses the creek, passes some bamboo groves, and ends at a second creek. This marks the end of the park trail system, and from here it's a quick hike back toward the parking lot. Don't forget to stop by the arts center on your way back to take a look at the work of local artists.

Miles and Directions

0.0 Begin at the trailhead to the left of the Sertoma Arts Center.

0.2 Bear right to begin the loop trail. Be on the lookout for great blue herons, hawks, ducks, geese, and seagulls.

0.5 Trail bends left and continues along the lake. A trail to the right leads to the spillway and alternate parking.

1.2 At the intersection bear left.

1.3 Turn left just after the footbridge.

2.0 Climb up the wooden overlook tower for a nice view of the lake and boardwalk. Cross the boardwalk. Waterfowl love to hang out here.

2.1 Return to the beginning of the loop. Bear right to return the way you came.

2.2 Turn right to follow Lake Park Trail along a small creek. Bamboo groves line this quiet wooded stroll.

2.4 End of trail; turn around.

2.7 Arrive back at Shelley Lake Trail, turn right.

2.8 Arrive back at the trailhead at the parking lot.

2 Secret Creek Trail to Lake Access Road

This quick hike takes you through the highlights of Durant Nature Park in less than a mile. Begin with a stroll on the banks of Secret Creek, then visit the picnic area, playground, and boathouse. Finally, make your way to the Bird and Butterfly Garden and the Training Lodge. The trail ends at the parking lot near additional trailheads, giving you the option to continue exploring the park's 5 miles of interconnecting trails on your own.

Distance: 0.8-mile loop

Approximate hiking time: 45–60 minutes

Difficulty: Easy, with a few gentle hills

Trail surface: A forested trail and a paved access road

Best season: Summer

Other trail users: Joggers, dog walkers

Canine compatibility: Leashed dogs permitted

Fees and permits: No fees or permits required

Schedule: 8:00 a.m.– dusk

Water availability: Fountain

Maps: USGS Wake Forest, NC; trail map available at the trailhead

Jurisdiction: City of Raleigh Parks and Recreation Department

Trail contacts: Durant Nature Park, 8305 Camp Durant Road, Raleigh 27614; (919) 870-2871; www.raleighnc.gov

Finding the trailhead: From Interstate 540 take the Falls of the Neuse Road exit. Go 1 mile and turn right onto Durant Road. Go 1.5 miles and turn right onto Camp Durant Road. This road dead-ends into the park. The trailhead is beside a kiosk to the right of the park office. *DeLorme: North Carolina Atlas & Gazetteer:* Page 40 B3. GPS Coordinates: 35° 53' 39.3" N / 78° 34' 41.4" W

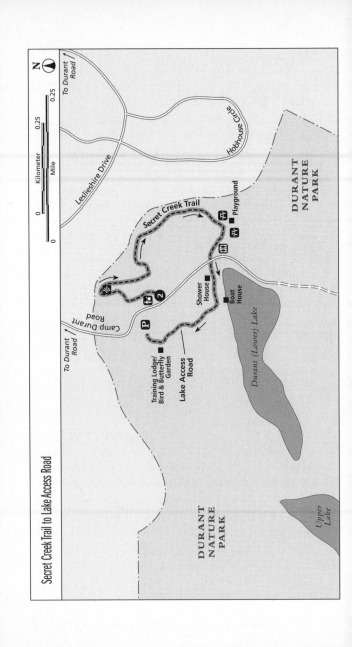

Secret Creek Trail to Lake Access Road

The Hike

Located in suburban north Raleigh, Durant Nature Park covers 237 acres surrounding two small lakes. The 5 miles of wide, interconnecting trails are a popular destination for local dog owners.

This nature park features a playground, large open fields, picnic areas, and a boathouse. Some of the trails are wheelchair accessible, primarily the area around the Training Lodge and Bird and Butterfly Garden. During warmer months the gardens bloom with indigenous flowers, attracting a variety of butterflies. Bird feeders are stocked year-round, with benches nearby where you can relax and observe some of the 160 bird species recorded at the park.

There are many ways to explore the 5 miles of trails, but this short route starts at the northeastern corner and ends near additional trailheads. Start with Secret Creek Trail, a relatively narrow path running alongside the creek, and one of the most serene trails in the park.

Begin Secret Creek Trail from the service road by the park office, and follow the trail down to the creek. Turn right along the banks and follow the creek for about 0.5 mile. You can see the Raleigh Greenway following the other side of the creek.

Along the trail, informational signposts identify many of the tree species, including poplar and red oak. Some large specimens of red cedar are particularly notable. Listen for the sound of woodpeckers, and note the many trees here with woodpecker holes.

In the creek and along the trail there are large, flat rocks—good places from which to spot crayfish and even salamanders.

Soon the trail leaves the creek and emerges in a large field just below the lake. Pass the playground and picnic shelters, heading up toward the lake. As you reach the lake, you'll see the boathouse and designated swimming area.

From the lake, follow the Lake Access Road up the hill and you'll reach the Training Lodge, used for special events and classes. The seasonal Bird and Butterfly Garden surrounds the lodge.

The parking lot is within sight of the lodge. If you'd like to continue exploring the park on your own, the trail continues down White House Road, into the center of the park, where you can access all of the other loop trails. The large loops are popular and worth taking the time to explore. Wildlife viewing may be spotty on busy days, but if you observe closely, you may see the tracks of deer, raccoons, beavers, and opossums near the banks.

Miles and Directions

0.0 Find the trailhead near the kiosk by the park office (off the service road).

0.1 Turn right at the intersection when you reach the creek.

0.3 Continue along stream.

0.5 End of Secret Creek Trail. Emerge from woods near picnic shelters and playground. Take the paved path to the right toward the lake.

0.6 Keep straight, passing the shower house on your right. After the shower house bear right. You'll pass the boathouse on your left.

0.7 Stroll uphill toward the Training Lodge and Bird and Butterfly Garden. Stop to enjoy the garden.

0.8 Keep straight at the intersection. Return to trailhead at the parking lot, or from here choose one of the other trailheads leading into the park.

3 Lake Johnson Park

This hike begins with an easy wooded walk around the western side of Lake Johnson, then strikes out on a paved path to tour the eastern side. The last leg of the hike is a rugged footpath that closely follows the lakeside and features excellent views. The park's interconnecting trails make it easy to choose alternate routes to suit any hiker.

Distance: 4.9-mile figure-eight
Approximate hiking time: 3-4 hours
Difficulty: Moderate due to varied terrain with some hills
Trail surface: Paved forested trails and unpaved forested trails
Best seasons: Spring and fall
Other trail users: Mountain bikers, joggers, dog walkers
Canine compatibility: Leashed dogs permitted
Fees and permits: No fees or permits required

Schedule: Dawn to dusk. Closed on Thanksgiving Day, December 24 and 25, January 1, and Martin Luther King Jr. Day.
Water availability: Fountain and seasonal concession stand
Maps: USGS Raleigh West, NC; trail map available at trailhead
Jurisdiction: City of Raleigh Parks and Recreation Department
Trail contacts: Lake Johnson Park, 4601 Avent Ferry Road, Raleigh 27606; (919) 233-2121; www.raleighnc.gov

Finding the trailhead: From Interstate 40 East take exit 295 (Gorman Street). Turn right onto Gorman Street. At the first light turn right onto Tryon Road. Drive for about 1 mile, then turn right onto Avent Ferry Road. Drive about 0.7 mile and turn right into the alternate parking lot. (The main parking lot by the boathouse is a farther 0.3 mile up Avent Ferry Road if the alternate lot is full.) Trailheads are located in both parking lots at the kiosks. *DeLorme: North Carolina Atlas & Gazetteer:* Page 40 C2. GPS Coordinates: 35° 45' 33.8" N / 78° 43' 01.2" W

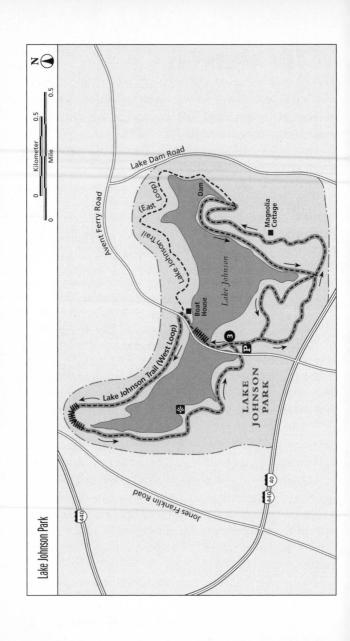

Lake Johnson Park

The Hike

The 5.5 miles of paved and unpaved trails at Lake Johnson Park are an opportunity for beginners and experienced hikers alike to enjoy nature. The diversity of the trails is this park's most striking characteristic.

As with other Raleigh city parks, Lake Johnson's paved trails connect to the Raleigh Greenway system, ensuring steady foot and bike traffic at most times. The unpaved trails are more serene and offer the best nature walks.

Lake Johnson Park features a boathouse with a variety of small boats available for rental. A concession stand, bathrooms, and live bait sales are also available here.

The park's primary trail is the Lake Johnson Trail, divided into the East Loop and West Loop. The East Loop is mostly paved and is part of the Raleigh Greenway. The West Loop is mostly unpaved.

Beginning from the alternate parking lot, the trail takes you to the park's main boardwalk, where you'll immediately have a great view of the lake. Take the boardwalk to the boathouse, and cross the road to the park's unpaved West Loop. The trail is flat and wide for the first mile.

At the far western end of the lake, a second boardwalk takes you across a marshy area where waterfowl and other wildlife are common. The trail then begins to climb and becomes narrower. An overlook with a bench provides a good viewing opportunity of the western side of the lake.

The West Loop returns to the parking area. From here you can take the flight of steps to the paved East Loop. The East Loop is family friendly, but hilly, with some fairly steep grades.

If you prefer the paved trail, you may remain on the East

Loop and return to the boardwalk via the boathouse. Otherwise, after a little over a mile on the paved trail, you can take a hard left onto an unpaved trail that follows the lakeside more closely. This route is more rugged but generally less crowded than the Greenway trails, with better views.

A few species less common to the Raleigh-Durham area inhabit Lake Johnson. Yucca can be spotted along the banks, and the distinctive trill of the belted kingfisher can be heard all around the lake.

Miles and Directions

0.0 Begin at the trailhead by the large kiosk in the parking lot. Bear left at the first intersection.

0.1 Cross the boardwalk over Lake Johnson.

0.3 Turn left at the intersection and cross the street.

0.5 Continue straight at the intersection.

0.7 Continue straight at the intersection.

0.9 Continue straight at the intersection.

1.0 Turn left onto the boardwalk.

1.6 Continue straight at the next two intersections.

2.1 Cross the street and walk to the parking lot where you started. For a shorter hike you can end here.

2.2 At the far end of the parking lot, climb the flight of stairs. This side of the lake has paved trails. Bear right at the next two closely spaced intersections.

2.3 Continue straight at the intersection.

2.7 Continue straight at the intersection.

2.9 Bear right at the next two intersections (a small loop breaks off to the left, then rejoins the trail).

3.4 Make a sharp left onto an unmarked, unpaved trail. Keep out a sharp eye for this turn as it almost doubles back. The turnoff is just before the paved East Loop itself makes a sharp bend to the left. Follow this trail along the shore.

4.2 Bear right at the intersection at the foot of the hill, crossing the creek at the rocks.

4.5 At the top of the hill, return to the paved loop trail. On your right is a nice overlook. Turn left to head home.

4.6 Bear right at the intersection.

4.7 Bear right at the next two intersections.

4.8 Turn left at the intersection.

4.9 Return to the stairs leading to the parking lot and trailhead.

4 Sal's Branch Trail

Sal's Branch Trail is a great introduction to the 22 miles of hiking trails at William B. Umstead State Park. This loop trail runs downhill through pine forest and mixed hardwood forest. The far end of the loop passes Big Lake, where you can stop to rent a canoe, or just explore the banks before heading back uphill through beech forest. Take note of the quartz deposits common in the park.

Distance: 2.5-mile loop
Approximate hiking time: 60–90 minutes
Difficulty: Moderate due to some rough, rooty sections
Trail surface: Forested trail
Best seasons: Spring and fall
Other trail users: Joggers, dog walkers
Canine compatibility: Leashed dogs permitted
Fees and permits: No fees or permits required
Schedule: November–February: 8:00 a.m.– 6:00 p.m.; March–

May and September–October: 8:00 a.m.–8:00 p.m.; June–August: 8:00 a.m.–9:00 p.m. Closed on December 25.
Water availability: None
Maps: USGS Southeast Durham and Cary, NC; trail map available at trailhead
Jurisdiction: NC Division of Parks and Recreation
Trail contacts: William B. Umstead State Park, 8801 Glenwood Avenue, Raleigh 27617; (919) 571-4170; www.ncparks .gov/Visit/parks/wium/main.php

Finding the trailhead: From U.S. Highway 70/Glenwood Avenue, take the Interstate 540E exit. Drive 1.5 miles to the park's Crabtree Creek entrance on your right. From the entrance, drive about 0.5 mile and turn right into the visitor center parking lot. The trailhead is located to the right of the visitor center by the kiosk. *DeLorme: North Carolina Atlas & Gazetteer:* Page 40 B1. GPS Coordinates: 35° 52' 51.4" N / 78° 45' 30.4" W

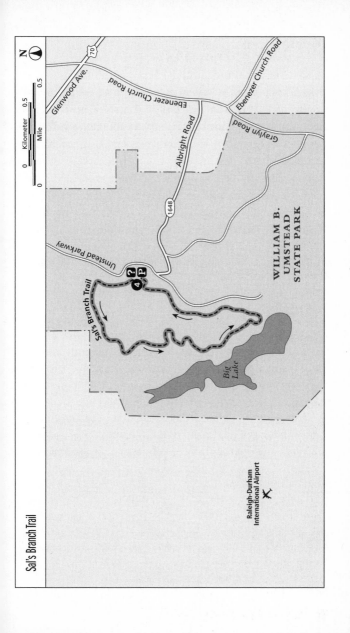

Sal's Branch Trail

The Hike

William B. Umstead State Park is one of the oldest and best-known parks in the Raleigh-Durham area. Covering some 5,500 acres, this expansive park is a great destination for most outdoor activities. Car camping, boating, and horseback riding are popular here. The park also features 22 miles of hiking trails.

Sal's Branch Trail is a perfect introduction to the park. Beginning at an upland section by the visitor center, you'll head downhill, crossing creeks. The trail itself is well maintained but rough in places, with many tree roots and rocks. Along the way you'll see rocky ridges with prominent quartz deposits, common in the area. Look for the remains of a low stone wall near the first footbridge. Such traces of early settlements are found throughout the park.

The trail emerges from the woods at Big Lake. Canoes are available for rental here, and the lake is a good place to view waterfowl for most of the year.

The final leg of the loop winds back up through a predominantly beech forest before returning to the visitor center.

Umstead provides many additional opportunities for hikers to explore. From Big Lake the trailhead branches out into the park, and there are several other parking areas that provide access to different points in the network of trails. The 22-mile network features a mill site, campgrounds, and two smaller lakes.

Miles and Directions

0.0 Begin at the trailhead just past the kiosk to the right of the visitor center. Bear right onto the loop trail.

0.1 Cross the footbridge.

0.4 Continue straight at the intersection.

1.7 Trail emerges from the woods with a view of Big Lake. Bear left to follow Sal's Branch Trail back upland into the woods.

2.4 Bear left at the intersection.

2.5 Bear right to leave the loop trail and return to the trailhead.

5 Laurel Cliffs Nature Trail

This short self-guided nature hike offers an introduction to some of the region's most important plant species. The trail begins with a wooded uphill climb and ends at the Laurel Cliffs with a spectacular view of the Eno River. A free guide available at the trailhead helps interpret the informational trail markers. This is a great hike for families, who may want to explore the other attractions offered at West Point on the Eno Park.

Distance: 0.4-mile point-to-point
Approximate hiking time: 20–30 minutes
Difficulty: Moderate due to some short rocky sections
Trail surface: Forested trail
Best seasons: Spring and fall
Other trail users: Joggers, dog walkers
Canine compatibility: Leashed dogs permitted
Fees and permits: No fees or permits required

Schedule: 8:00 a.m.– dusk
Water availability: Fountain
Maps: USGS Northwest Durham, NC; trail map available at the kiosks
Jurisdiction: City of Durham Parks and Recreation Department
Trail contacts: West Point on the Eno Park, 5101 North Roxboro Road, Durham 27704; (919) 471-1623; www.durhamnc.gov/departments/parks/parks.cfm

Finding the trailhead: From Interstate 85 South in Durham, take the Duke Street exit and turn right onto Duke Street. Follow Duke Street for about 2.3 miles, then continue on North Roxboro Road. Follow North Roxboro for about 1 mile. Turn left at the park entrance at the Seven Oaks Road stoplight. Keep right and follow the signs to the parking lot. Take a short walk to the left, along the gravel road. The Laurel Cliffs Nature trailhead is on your right, across from the picnic shelter. *DeLorme: North Carolina Atlas & Gazetteer:* Page 39 A7. GPS Coordinates: 36° 04' 10.6" N / 78° 54' 36.6" W

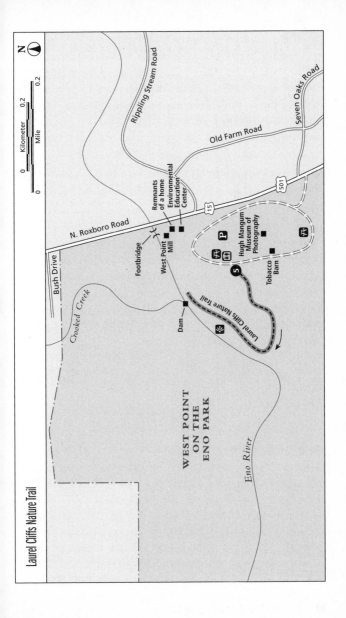

Laurel Cliffs Nature Trail

N

0   0.2
Kilometer
0   0.2
Mile

Bush Drive

Crooked Creek

Rippling Stream Road

Old Farm Road

Seven Oaks Road

Remnants of a home

Environmental Education Center

N. Roxboro Road

Footbridge

West Point Mill

15

501

P

Hugh Mangum Museum of Photography

Tobacco Barn

5

Dam

Laurel Cliffs Nature Trail

WEST POINT ON THE ENO PARK

Eno River

The Hike

West Point on the Eno Park is best known for its recon-structed eighteenth-century gristmill. From 1778 until it shut down in 1942, the mill was the economic center of the small community of West Point. Several other historic structures still remain, housing a photography museum, park office, and frequent weekend events. These attrac-tions, as well as ample parking, picnic facilities, and wide, open spaces, make West Point a terrific place for a family outing.

West Point offers so many diversions that visitors could almost overlook the excellent hiking opportunities on 3.5 miles of trails. There is a lot to explore here along the Eno River and in the surrounding woodlands.

One of the park's highlights is the Laurel Cliffs along the river's south bank. Here you'll be treated to one of the best scenic views of the Eno in Durham. To reach the cliffs, take the Laurel Cliffs Nature Trail, a short scenic hike with sixteen trail markers highlighting important plant species and landmarks. A free guide is available at the trailhead to help interpret these markers.

The first leg of the trip is a gentle uphill climb. There are several benches along the route, so hikers of any skill level can take their time enjoying the scenery. The scenic trail markers will tend to lengthen the time spent on this short trail. The trail is well marked. The biggest hazard here is an abundance of tree roots, so watch your step!

On the final leg of the hike, just after the Eno River overlook, there is a short but somewhat steep rocky descent. If this appears too difficult, you will miss very little by turn-ing back now and retracing your steps.

After you descend, the trail ends at the dam, adjacent to one of the park's picnic areas. The main parking lot is within sight across the road. From the dam you will also have a good view of the West Point Mill, which is open to visitors on weekends.

Miles and Directions

0.0 Cross the footbridge to the trailhead. Make sure to take a Nature Guide as you begin your hike.

0.1 Turn left at the T intersection (follow the yellow arrow).

0.1 Stay right at the unmarked intersection.

0.2 Turn right at the T intersection (follow the yellow arrow).

0.3 Enjoy the scenic river overlook. Look for deer on the grassy north bank. If the next section looks too rocky, you can still turn back here for a less steep descent.

0.4 Arrive at the end of the trail next to the West Point Dam. The historic West Point Mill is within sight, as are the parking lot and trailhead.

6 Blue Jay Point County Park

This loop trail begins with a self-guided interpretive hike, then strikes out for the shore of Falls Lake. Follow the lakeside, stopping for a great view before heading back for home. Wildflowers are especially common in spring months, and a garden area features native plants selected to attract wildlife.

Distance: 2.2-mile loop
Approximate hiking time: 1–2 hours
Difficulty: Moderate due to some steep switchbacks
Trail surface: Forested trail
Best seasons: Winter and spring
Other trail users: Joggers, dog walkers
Canine compatibility: Leashed dogs permitted
Fees and permits: No fees or permits required
Schedule: 8:00 a.m.–sunset. Closed Thanksgiving Day, December 24 and 25, and January 1.
Water availability: Fountain
Maps: USGS Bayleaf, NC; trail map available at the trailhead
Jurisdiction: Wake County Parks, Recreation and Open Space (PROS) Department
Trail contacts: Blue Jay Point County Park, 3200 Pleasant Union Church Road, Raleigh 27614; (919) 870-4330; www .wakegov.com/parks/bluejay/ default.htm

Finding the trailhead: From Interstate 40 take the Interstate 540 East exit. Drive about 10 miles and take exit 11 (Six Forks Road). Turn left onto Six Forks Road. Drive 2.8 miles, then turn left to continue onto Six Forks Road. Drive 1.6 miles and turn right onto Pleasant Union Church Road. Park in the first parking lot on the left (by the Blue Jay Center for Environmental Education). The trailhead begins next to the Blue Jay Center. *DeLorme: North Carolina Atlas & Gazetteer:* Page 40 B2. GPS Coordinates: 35° 58' 05.5" N / 78° 38' 37.3" W

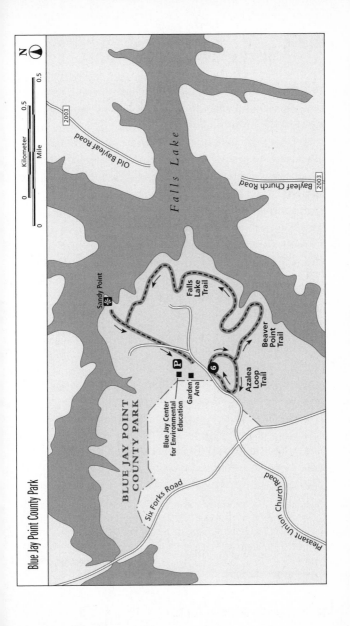

Blue Jay Point County Park

The Hike

Blue Jay Point County Park covers a 236-acre peninsula on Falls Lake. The park's longest trail is a 4-mile section of Falls Lake Trail, which itself extends beyond the park and is a part of the Mountains-to-Sea Trail.

Once mostly agricultural land, Blue Jay Point now consists mainly of second-growth forest. Educational programs are a priority for the park and are held throughout the year. The large environmental education center adjacent to the main parking lot holds a Discovery Room and exhibits on the water cycle and the local watershed.

From the environmental education center, hike past the Blue Jay Garden and across the road to begin the Azalea Loop Trail. This self-guided hike features seasonal interpretive markers that showcase the various plant species and habitats common in the park.

The Azalea Loop Trail intersects Beaver Point Trail, a remnant of an old farm road. After a short walk down Beaver Point Trail turn left onto Falls Lake Trail. The hike continues along the lake for a little over a mile, departing from the banks in some areas in search of higher ground. The trail has some rough areas and moderate hills as it turns away from marshy areas.

Finally, Falls Lake Trail intersects with a smaller loop trail leading to a playground and picnic areas. Continue past these until you reach the Sandy Point Trail. A quick detour to the right takes you to Sandy Point, with a nice view of the lake.

Turn around and continue on the Falls Lake Trail back toward the parking lot. When you emerge at the alternate lot, cross the road and bear left. The main parking lot and environmental education center are within sight.

Miles and Directions

0.0 From the parking lot, hike toward the Blue Jay Center for Environmental Education. Pass the Blue Jay Garden area and cross the street to begin the Azalea Loop Trail. Turn left at the first intersection just after crossing the road.

0.2 At the T intersection turn right to continue the Azalea Loop Trail. You can turn left instead to cut out the last half of the Azalea Loop.

0.3 Turn right just before reaching the road.

0.4 Return to the beginning of the Azalea Loop Trail. Turn right, repeating a short section of the loop.

0.6 Return to the T intersection, this time turning left onto Beaver Point Trail.

0.7 Turn left onto Falls Lake Trail as you get within sight of Falls Lake.

1.4 Continue straight at intersection.

1.5 Bear right at the wooden railing. The trail leads downhill and across a footbridge.

1.6 Just after the footbridge bear right to continue on Falls Lake Trail. Continue straight at the intersection, then bear right, following the white blazes. Yellow blazes indicate the Laurel Loop Trail, which joins the Falls Lake Trail briefly.

1.9 Reach a T intersection. Turn right to check out Sandy Point, a nice place to get a view of the lake.

2.0 Return to the T intersection, headed away from the lake.

2.1 Arrive at the alternate parking lot. Cross the road and continue a short distance toward the main parking lot where you began.

2.2 Arrive back at the trailhead.

7 Johnston Mill Nature Preserve

This former homestead area is predominantly flat, with a series of bluffs as you head south. The bluffs can be bypassed for an easier hike, but to fully appreciate this diverse forest you'll want to climb the hill to reach the overlook. Dozens of tree species can be found in the preserve. Take your time and look for placards on many trees, a great introduction to tree identification.

Distance: 2.8-mile out-and-back
Approximate hiking time: 2 hours
Difficulty: Moderate due to some steep climbs
Trail surface: Forested trail
Best seasons: Spring and fall
Other trail users: Joggers, dog walkers
Canine compatibility: Leashed dogs permitted
Fees and permits: No fees or permits required

Schedule: Dawn to dusk
Water availability: None
Maps: USGS Chapel Hill, NC; trail map available at the trailhead
Jurisdiction: Triangle Land Conservancy
Trail contacts: Triangle Land Conservancy, 1101 Haynes Street, Suite 205, Raleigh 27604; (919) 833-3662; www.triangleland.org/lands/places_to_visit.shtml

Finding the trailhead: From Interstate 40 take exit 266 (Highway 86 North) and turn right. Drive 1.8 miles, then turn right onto Mount Sinai Road (just before the railroad tracks). Drive 1.1 miles and turn right into the parking lot immediately before the bridge. The trailhead is at the end of the parking lot. *DeLorme: North Carolina Atlas & Gazetteer:* Page 39 B6. GPS Coordinates: 35° 59' 43.1" N / 79° 03' 14.3" W

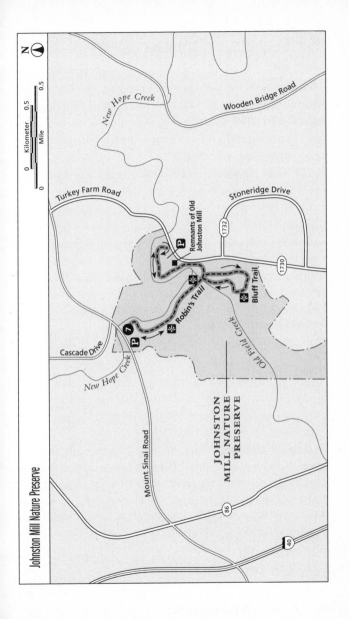

Johnston Mill Nature Preserve

The Hike

Johnston Mill Nature Preserve, formerly a homestead to the Johnston family for two centuries, was acquired by the Triangle Land Conservancy in 1999 and opened to the public in 2001. The 296-acre preserve is notable for its variety of tree species, many of which bear informational placards to aid identification.

This area is home to rare plant and animal species including the four-toed salamander and the green violet. More than 125 bird species have been recorded in the preserve.

Remnants of the old homestead can be found here, including stone walls, foundations, and two mill sites.

Highlights along the trail include a series of bluffs and a long boardwalk over a swampy area on the eastern side. The preserve's trails are generally well maintained, but rain and heavy traffic can cause some problems with mud.

In dry weather Johnston Mill is a great place to enjoy a nature walk. Robin's Trail is mostly flat and easy, with a couple of moderate climbs. Much of the forest in the flat areas is secondary growth returning after agricultural use.

Midway through the hike Robin's Trail intersects with the Bluff Trail loop. Hikers who would prefer an easier hike should stay on Robin's Trail, but those who don't mind a long uphill climb will enjoy the view of the woods from the bluffs. As you ascend, you'll notice more mature hardwood forests than you'll see on Robin's Trail. As you descend the bluffs, a shady section near the creek is a good place to look for ferns and other plant life you may not notice in other areas of the preserve.

Miles and Directions

0.0 Begin your hike at the well-marked trailhead.

0.3 Just before ascending a hill, stop to see a scenic rocky bend in New Hope Creek.

0.4 Continue straight at the intersection.

0.5 Bear left at the fork and cross the footbridge.

0.6 At the marked intersection, continue straight onto the Bluff Trail loop. Alternately, you can turn left to stay on Robin's Trail and avoid the rocky loop.

1.0 Stop at the overlook, where you can get an excellent view of Old Field Creek. Look for deer and other wildlife in this open area.

1.2 Return to the Bluff Trail loop intersection. Continue straight onto Robin's Trail.

1.4 As you pass the creek, look for the low rock wall (the remnants of Old Johnston Mill).

1.7 Cross a boardwalk over a swampy area. Look for changes in flora and fauna.

1.7 Reach the Turkey Farm Road parking lot. Retrace your steps to return to the Mount Sinai Road parking lot.

2.8 Arrive back at the trailhead.

8 Historic Yates Mill County Park

Yates Mill Park is one of the most pristine parks in the region and is home to a breathtaking diversity of plant and animal species. Begin your hike by crossing the pond boardwalk and exploring the nearby wetlands. Then return to the pond, where you'll discover historic Yates Mill, the only operational gristmill in Wake County.

Distance: 2.8- to 3.0-mile loop
Approximate hiking time: 2 hours
Difficulty: Moderate due to varied terrain
Trail surface: Forested trails and boardwalks
Best seasons: Winter and spring
Other trail users: Joggers
Canine compatibility: No dogs permitted
Fees and permits: No fees or permits required
Schedule: 8:00 a.m.–sunset. Closed Thanksgiving Day, December 24 and 25, and January 1.
Water availability: None
Maps: USGS Lake Wheeler, NC; trail map available at trailhead
Jurisdiction: Wake County Parks, Recreation and Open Space (PROS) Department
Trail contacts: Historic Yates Mill County Park, 4620 Lake Wheeler Road, Raleigh 27603; (919) 856-6675; www.wakegov.com/parks/yatesmill/default.htm

---

Finding the trailhead: From Interstate 40 East, take exit 295 (Gorman Street). Turn right onto Gorman Street. Then turn right onto Tryon Road at the light. Drive 1.3 miles and turn right onto Lake Wheeler Road. Drive 1.6 miles on Lake Wheeler Road. The park is on your right. *DeLorme: North Carolina Atlas & Gazetteer:* Page 40 D2. GPS Coordinates: 35° 43' 14.0" N / 78° 41' 15.7" W

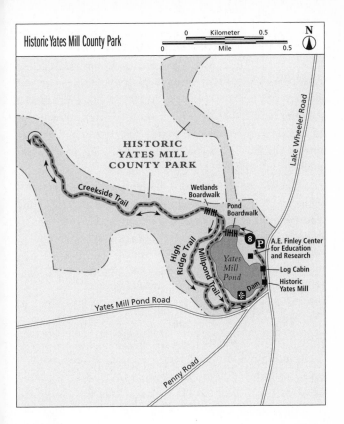

Kilometer

Mile

N

HISTORIC
YATES MILL
COUNTY PARK

Creekside Trail

Wetlands
Boardwalk

Pond
Boardwalk

High Ridge Trail

Millpond Trail

Yates
Mill
Pond

8

P

A.E. Finley Center
for Education
and Research

Log Cabin

Historic
Yates Mill

Dam

Yates Mill Pond Road

Lake Wheeler Road

Penny Road

The Hike

Surrounded by farmland, Historic Yates Mill County Park is home to healthy plant and wildlife populations. Half a dozen large informational kiosks throughout the park showcase the great variety of life found here, including animals such as the bobcat, river otter, and red fox.

The park's biodiversity is in part due to its geographical variety. On only 574 acres the park contains a large 20-acre pond, high ridges, low wetlands, and creeks. Due to the park's significance as a wildlife refuge, pets are not allowed.

Begin your hike at the boardwalk, with a good view of the pond. Viewing scopes, found here and at other locations in the park, help you check out the local scenery and wildlife.

Continue to the second boardwalk over the wetlands section of the pond. This is possibly the best area of the park for wildlife viewing. Watch out for beavers, hawks, and other pond life.

The wetlands boardwalk leads to the 1-mile Creekside Trail, which leads into the wetlands along the park's edge. Many footbridges and boardwalks make this fairly easy going. The park has plans to extend this trail in the future, but for now it ends in a short loop before returning. This unspoiled area is a good place for bird-watching.

Returning from the Creekside Trail, hikers are presented with the option to follow the Millpond Trail around the pond, or to take the High Ridge Trail for part of the distance. From the ridge trail you'll have an view of the wetlands to the west and the pond to the east.

As you round the southern end of the pond, you'll reach a picnic area and an observation platform before finally reaching Historic Yates Mill.

Like West Point in Durham, Yates Mill is on the National Register of Historic Places, was reconstructed from the remnants of the original eighteenth-century mill, and still operates today. This is the only working gristmill in Wake County.

Miles and Directions

0.0 Begin at the pond boardwalk to the right of the visitor center.

0.1 Just after the pond boardwalk, turn right at the intersection.

0.2 Continue straight at the intersection and cross the wetlands boardwalk. Excellent wildlife viewing opportunities here.

0.3 Begin the Creekside Trail. Cross a dozen small footbridges and boardwalks as you make your way through the wetlands.

1.1 The trail terminates in a small loop. A sign indicates the end of the trail. The trail bends to the left of the sign and turns back.

1.2 The loop returns to the trail. Turn right to continue heading back.

2.1 Cross the wetlands boardwalk once again. Continue straight at the intersection to begin the Millpond Trail. Alternately, turn right to follow the High Ridge Trail, a more challenging route that joins Millpond Trail farther down. (This route adds 0.2 mile.)

2.2 Bear right to follow Millpond Trail around the pond.

2.5 Continue straight at the intersection. This is where High Ridge Trail rejoins Millpond Trail.

2.6 Reach an overlook platform with another great view of the pond.

2.7 The trail passes Yates Mill and a log cabin. Guided tours of the mill are available certain times of the year.

2.8 Arrive back at the trailhead.

9 Hemlock Bluffs Nature Preserve

This beautiful preserve in southern Cary is one of the few places where you can see mountain plant species in the Piedmont. Begin your hike with the short Swift Creek Loop Trail, which offers magnificent views as it descends the bluffs. Then take a short walk to the Chestnut Oak Loop Trail, a longer wooded hike with several more scenic overlooks. Free nature guides available at the trailhead provide background information about the preserve's ecology.

Distance: 1.9-mile double loop

Approximate hiking time: 2–3 hours

Difficulty: Moderate due to some steep stairs on the bluffs

Trail surface: Forested trail and boardwalks

Best season: Spring

Other trail users: Joggers, dog walkers

Canine compatibility: Leashed dogs permitted

Fees and permits: No fees or permits required

Schedule: 9:00 a.m.–dusk

Water availability: None

Maps: USGS Apex, NC; trail map available at trailhead

Jurisdiction: Cary Parks, Recreation, and Cultural Resources Department

Trail contacts: Hemlock Bluffs Nature Preserve, P.O. Box 8005 Cary, NC 27512; (919) 387-5980; www.townofcary.org/depts/prdept/parks/hemlock.htm

Finding the trailhead: From Interstate 40 take exit 293 to U.S. Highway 64 West/U.S. Highway 1 South. From US 64 West/US 1 South, take exit 98A onto Tryon Road. At the third light, turn right onto Kildaire Farm Road. In about 1.5 miles, the Hemlock Bluffs Nature Preserve will be on your right. From the parking lot, follow the path to the Stevens Nature Center. The trailhead starts in front of the Center. *DeLorme: North Carolina Atlas & Gazetteer:* Page 40 D1. GPS Coordinates: 35° 43' 26.9" N / 78° 47' 01.7" W

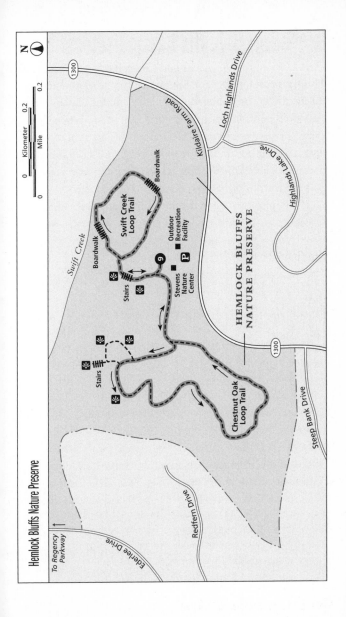

Hemlock Bluffs Nature Preserve

N

Swift Creek

Boardwalk

Boardwalk

Swift Creek Loop Trail

Boardwalk

Stairs

Outdoor Recreation Facility

9

Stevens Nature Center

P

Stairs

Stairs

Chestnut Oak Loop Trail

HEMLOCK BLUFFS NATURE PRESERVE

Kildaire Farm Road

Loch Highlands Drive

Highlands Lake Drive

1300

1300

Steep Bank Drive

Redfern Drive

Ederlee Drive

To Regency Parkway

0   Kilometer   0.2

0   Mile   0.2

The Hike

Hemlock Bluffs Nature Preserve is named for its stand of eastern hemlocks, a species normally indigenous to the mountains. The eastern bluffs overlooking Swift Creek provide a cool, moist microclimate where mountain species thrive. This was a typical ecology in this area thousands of years ago during the last glacial period, and the bluffs have provided a small niche for these species to survive here, over 200 miles from what is now their normal range.

The trails here are wide and well maintained. The beautiful Stevens Nature Center is the first thing you will see when you arrive at the park. The nature center features a native wildflower garden, as well as classrooms and exhibits. The surrounding gardens and first trail segments are wheelchair accessible, but the loop trails themselves are not, as they have stairs and some rough patches.

The bluffs offer some incredible views. The forest canopies can be seen from above in many places, and the unique plant life found here contributes to a diverse bird population.

The Swift Creek Loop Trail descends the bluffs to view the mountain species up close. The longer Chestnut Oak Loop Trail explores the upland portion of the park and contains mixed hardwood/pine forest more typical of the region.

From the trailhead, pick up a nature guide and turn right toward the Swift Creek Loop Trail. The first overlook is just a minute's walk from the trailhead. A long staircase descends the bluffs, attached to two large overlook areas featuring plenty of benches.

At the bottom of the stairs you'll begin the loop. Keep left to follow the markers in the nature guide. As you walk alongside Swift Creek and over boardwalks, be on the lookout above and below for birds and river animals. The large boxes on some of the trees are wood duck nesting boxes. Owls, foxes, muskrats, and beavers may also be seen here. Some exceptionally large American hollies overhang parts of the loop.

The loop returns to the base of the stairs. Ascend the bluffs once more and make the short walk back to the trailhead. For a shorter hike you can end here, turning left to return to the nature center, but you will miss some wonderful viewing opportunities at the overlooks on the Chestnut Oak Loop Trail.

Continue straight at the trailhead to reach the Chestnut Oak Loop and visit the upland portion of the park. Keep right at the fork and follow the loop. Optional side loops lead to viewing platforms on the western bluffs. The remainder of the Chestnut Oak Loop winds through the woods for less than a mile before returning to the trailhead.

Miles and Directions

0.0 Start at the trailhead by the Stevens Nature Center and turn right to head toward the Swift Creek Loop Trail. Don't forget to grab a trail guide! Soon you will reach the first overlook. Take the stairs down the bluffs.

0.1 Bear left at the intersection (this is the loop).

0.2 A boardwalk carries you over the swampy areas near the creek. Keep a lookout for wildlife.

0.3 Cross a small footbridge

0.4 A second boardwalk. Keep your eyes and ears open! Wildlife is abundant in this area.

0.6 Return to the beginning of the loop. Continue back up the stairs toward the trailhead.

0.7 Return to the trailhead and continue straight toward the Chestnut Oak Loop Trail.

0.9 Begin the loop. Bear right where the trail forks to follow the interpretive trail markers in order. Soon thereafter, at the next intersection, you may continue on Chestnut Oak Loop Trail or turn right to follow a short side loop leading to two scenic overlooks. (The loop trail adds 0.3 mile to your hike and has some steep hills.)

1.0 Turn left onto the footbridge. (It will be a right turn if you took the alternative loop.)

1.1 Scenic overlook of Swift Creek.

1.7 Return to the loop intersection. Continue straight to return to the nature center.

1.9 Reach the trailhead where you began your hike.

10 Lake Crabtree County Park–Lake Trail

This 5.8-mile loop trail around Lake Crabtree passes through woodlands, across an earthen dam, and through wetland areas. The hike's varied terrain includes some steep climbs, providing photographers and nature lovers with great views and diverse sights.

Distance: 5.8-mile loop

Approximate hiking time: 3–4 hours

Difficulty: Moderate due to some steep climbs and varied terrain

Trail surface: Forested trail

Best seasons: Spring and fall

Other trail users: Mountain bikers, joggers, dog walkers

Canine compatibility: Leashed dogs permitted

Fees and permits: No fees or permits required

Schedule: 8:00 a.m.– sunset. Closed Thanksgiving Day, December 24 and 25, and January 1.

Water availability: Fountain

Maps: USGS Cary, NC; trail map available at trailhead

Jurisdiction: Wake County Parks, Recreation and Open Space (PROS) Department

Trail contacts: Lake Crabtree County Park, 1400 Aviation Parkway, Morrisville 27560; (919) 460-3390; www.wakegov.com/parks/lakecrabtree/default.htm

Finding the trailhead: From Interstate 40 take exit 285 (Aviation Parkway). Head south on Aviation Parkway and turn left into the park in about 0.5 mile. Bear right at the fork, then take the second right. There are a number of parking areas. Park in the lot across the road from the manager's office. The trailhead is at the kiosk. *DeLorme: North Carolina Atlas & Gazetteer:* Page 40 B1. GPS Coordinates: 35° 50' 25.2" N / 78° 47' 34.2" W

Lake Crabtree County Park–Lake Trail

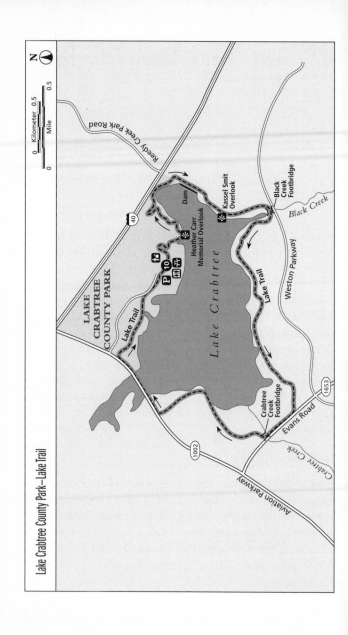

The Hike

This 5.8-mile trek around 520-acre Lake Crabtree begins with a hilly, wooded walk on the northern side of the lake. The trail soon emerges into an open area on the lake's eastern end and heads uphill toward the earthen dam.

The trail becomes paved at the dam, and here the park connects to the Raleigh Greenway system. Take a scenic walk over the dam and continue to a footbridge where the unpaved trail resumes.

The trail passes over some steep hills before settling into a flatter, easier area. As you reach the southern side of the lake, you pass through swampy areas. Keep an eye out for the gnawed trees and sticks indicating beaver activity in this section.

Skirting the highway, you'll return to drier woods on the western side of the lake. This end of the lake is shallow and a good place to spot waterfowl.

The final leg of the hike alternates between swampy areas and open forest, finally becoming an open field near the end. The meadow is adjacent to a small parking area. From here you'll return to the park road and hike a short way back to the trailhead.

Miles and Directions

0.0 Find the trailhead kiosk at the parking lot across the road from the manager's office.

0.4 Continue straight at the intersection and pass the Heather Carr Memorial Overlook.

0.9 Turn right at the intersection, staying along the lake.

1.1 At the top of the hill, the trail meets the Raleigh Greenway and becomes paved. Bear right to stay in the park.

1.3 From the middle of the dam, you have an excellent view of the portion of the lake you've just hiked.

1.6 Pass the Kassel Smit Overlook.

1.8 Continue straight at the intersection.

1.9 Turn right onto the Black Creek footbridge, leaving the paved portion of the trail.

3.7 Cross over the Crabtree Creek footbridge.

3.9 Pass the Southport entrance to the park.

5.3 Arrive at the end of Lake Trail at the back of the open field. Walk across the field toward the parking lot.

5.4 Walk through the parking lot to the park road.

5.5 Follow the park road to your right to return to the trailhead.

5.8 Arrive back at the trailhead.

11 Ridge Trail to North River Trail

This hike features a moderate uphill climb that passes through different stages of forest succession, changing from young pine forests in the low areas to mature mixed hardwood on the bluffs by Little River. A loop trail at the end takes you along the river before heading back.

Distance: 3.3-mile lollipop

Approximate hiking time: 3 hours

Difficulty: Moderate due to some steep climbs

Trail surface: Forested trail

Best season: Spring

Other trail users: Joggers, dog walkers

Canine compatibility: Leashed dogs permitted

Fees and permits: No fees or permits required

Schedule: November 1–March 31: 8:00 a.m.–5:00 p.m.; June 1–August 31: 7:00 a.m.–8:00 p.m.; April 1–May 31 and September 1–October 31: 8:00 a.m.–6:00 p.m. Park is closed Thanksgiving Day, December 24 and 25.

Water availability: Fountain

Maps: USGS Rougemont, NC; trail map available at the trailhead

Jurisdiction: Orange County Recreation and Parks Department

Trail contacts: Central Recreation Center, 300 West Tryon Street, P.O. Box 8181 Hillsborough, NC 27278; (919) 245-2660; www.co.orange.nc .us/RecParks/little_river_park .asp

Finding the trailhead: From Interstate 85 take exit 175 (Guess Road). Drive north on Guess Road for about 10 miles. The park entrance is on the right (about 1 mile past the Orange County border). The trailhead is at the end of the parking lot. *DeLorme: North Carolina Atlas & Gazetteer:* Page 19 D7. GPS Coordinates: 36° 09' 44.6" N / 78° 58' 13.7" W

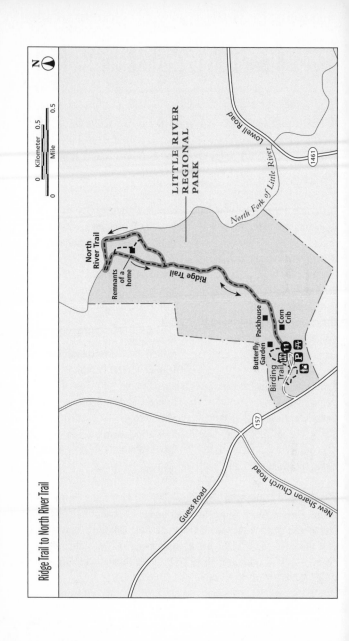

Ridge Trail to North River Trail

The Hike

Little River Regional Park is a popular destination for family outings, with playgrounds, gardens, a paved nature walk, a short birding trail, and ample picnic facilities.

The Ridge Trail provides a more adventurous experience, striking out for the far north of the park. The lower areas of the park were formerly cleared, so as you make your way up the Ridge Trail, you'll see forest succession in action.

The trail gradually climbs until it meets the North River Trail, a loop that runs down along the river. The high sections of the North River Trail provide a particularly scenic view of the river, and there are some impressive beech trees along the trail.

There are good wildlife viewing opportunities in the park. Notably, turkey and mink have been spotted in the area.

As you return along the Ridge Trail, there are several intersections branching into a network of trails in the southern part of the park that you can explore on your own. These interconnecting trails consist of the South River Loop Trail as well as 7 miles of mountain bike trails. Hiking is permitted on the bike trails, but hikers must yield to bikes.

Miles and Directions

0.0 Pass under the wooden structure (the Corn Crib) and continue straight down the trail into the woods.

0.3 Bear right where the trail forks just before the Packhouse. Bear left at the fork just after the Packhouse.

0.6 Continue straight at the intersection just after the boardwalk.

1.1 Cross the service road, then turn right onto North River Trail (post 39).

1.3 Continue straight on North River Trail.

1.4 The trail meets Little River.

1.8 Reach the top of a hill. From here you have a sweeping view of the surrounding land and river.

1.9 Continue straight (post 51).

2.2 Continue following North River Trail straight back the way you came.

3.0 Emerge from the woods by the Packhouse and bear right, then continue straight.

3.3 Return to the trailhead.

12 Pump Station Trail to Laurel Bluffs Trail

At the Pump Station access to Eno River State Park, you can explore the ruins of Durham's first pump station, then take a long walk along the banks of the Eno River. Along this rugged trail you'll see the remains of some of the earliest structures in Durham, including a dam, lodge, and Guess Mill. A varied geography makes this an interesting hike—you'll ascend cliffs over the river and pass through flat, shady meadows. The trail ends at Guess Road, where you can arrange for a ride or hike back toward the parking area.

Distance: 5.2-mile out-and-back (2.6 one way)
Approximate hiking time: 3–4 hours
Difficulty: Moderate due to some hills and rough trails
Trail surface: Forested trails
Best seasons: Spring and summer
Other trail users: Joggers, dog walkers
Canine compatibility: Leashed dogs permitted
Fees and permits: No fees or permits required
Schedule: May–August: 8:30 a.m.–8:30 p.m.; September and April: 8:30 a.m.–7:30 p.m.; March and October: 8:30 a.m.–6:30 p.m.; November–February: 8:30 a.m.–5:30 p.m.
Water availability: None
Maps: USGS Northwest Durham, NC; trail map available at trailhead
Jurisdiction: NC Division of Parks and Recreation
Trail contacts: Eno River State Park, 6101 Cole Mill Road, Durham 27705; (919) 383-1686; www.ncparks.gov/Visit/parks/enri/main.php

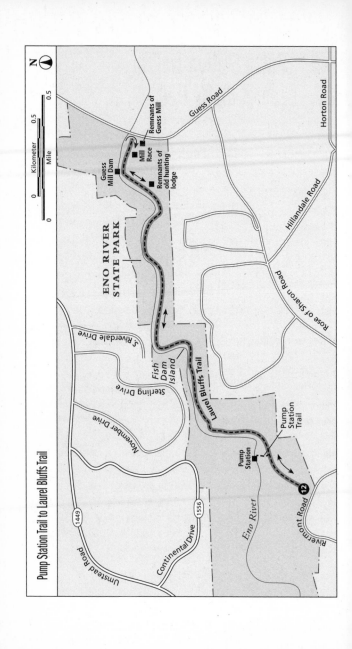

Pump Station Trail to Laurel Bluffs Trail

N

Remnants of Guess Mill

Guess Road

Mill Race

Guess Mill Dam

Remnants of old hunting lodge

ENO RIVER STATE PARK

S Riverdale Drive

Sterling Drive

November Drive

Fish Dam Island

Laurel Bluffs Trail

Rose of Sharon Road

Hillandale Road

Horton Road

Umstead Road

Continental Drive

1449

1556

Eno River

Pump Station

Pump Station Trail

12

Rivermont Road

Kilometer

Mile

0.5

0.5

Finding the trailhead: From Interstate 85 South in Durham, take the Cole Mill Road exit. Turn right (north) onto Cole Mill Road and travel about 2.5 miles. Turn right onto Rivermont Road and follow it until you cross a small bridge. Park along the road by the bridge. The trailhead is beside the bridge. *DeLorme: North Carolina Atlas & Gazetteer:* Page 39 A7. GPS Coordinates: 36° 03' 30.7" N / 78° 57' 56.3" W

The Hike

Eno River State Park covers 3,900 acres along 12 miles of the Eno River in Durham. This park has four separate access areas with a total of 24 miles of trails. The Pump Station access area is one of the smallest and least developed but is also one of the most interesting. This is the site of Durham's first pump station, which was the sole water supply to the city from 1887 to 1927. The ruins of the pump station still stand along the river. Other signs of abandoned structures, including a hunting lodge, dam, and mill, are scattered throughout the park. A sense of history is present along the trail as you pass old rock walls and foundations.

In springtime this is one of the best hikes for wildflowers, as the different altitudes, flat areas, and the humidity from the river provide a varied and fertile climate. On quiet days there are many wildlife viewing opportunities. The Eno River is mostly wide, shallow, and slow moving here, attracting herons, raccoons, crayfish, and other river species.

Begin your hike from the parking area by the bridge. Follow the trailhead down a portion of the Pump Station Trail. At the intersection you'll continue straight on the Laurel Bluffs Trail, but first take a few minutes to take a left toward the river and explore the ruins of the pump station.

Back on the trail, you'll continue straight for about 2 miles until you reach Guess Road. The old Guess Mill is your final landmark, very close to Guess Road. The old dam is still mostly intact, and the millstone lies alongside the trail.

Across Guess Road is an access to West Point on the Eno Park. The Mountains-to-Sea Trail is planned to extend along this trail. There is a path leading up to Guess Road where you can end your hike if you can arrange to be picked up. Otherwise, simply head back the way you came.

Miles and Directions

0.0 From the bridge, head down the path toward the river.

0.3 The hike will go straight at the intersection. However, take a quick detour to your left to check out the ruins of Durham's first pump station.

1.1 Fish Dam Island.

2.4 Remnants of the old hunting lodge and Guess Mill Dam.

2.6 Guess Mill. End of park. Turn around and go back the way you came.

5.2 Return to the trailhead.

13 Swift Creek Bluffs Nature Preserve

Swift Creek Bluffs is a twenty-three-acre nature preserve tucked away in southern Cary. The preserve extends along the south bank of a 0.5-mile section of Swift Creek, where the bank is dominated by a series of bluffs supporting a diverse ecology. This hike follows the creek toward the bluffs, ending with fantastic views of the surrounding landscape. The return leg crosses a boardwalk over a swampy area and passes through mature deciduous forest.

Distance: 1.2-mile loop

Approximate hiking time: 30–60 minutes

Difficulty: Moderate due to one steep climb

Trail surface: Forested trail

Best season: Spring

Other trail users: Joggers, dog walkers

Canine compatibility: Leashed dogs permitted

Fees and permits: No fees or permits required

Schedule: Dawn to dusk

Water availability: None

Maps: USGS Apex, NC; trail map available at trailhead

Jurisdiction: Triangle Land Conservancy

Trail contacts: Triangle Land Conservancy, 1101 Haynes Street, Raleigh 27604; (919) 833-3662; www.triangleland .org/lands/places_to_visit.shtml

Finding the trailhead: From Interstate 40 take exit 293 to U.S. Highway 64 West/U.S. Highway 1 South. On US 64 West/US 1 South, take exit 98A onto Tryon Road. At the third light, turn right onto Kildaire Farm Road. Go 2 miles and turn left onto Penny Road, then go another 2 miles and turn left onto Holly Springs Road. Go about 0.7 mile, and turn left into the small parking lot across from High Ridge Drive. Swift Creek Bluffs Nature Preserve will be immediately to your right in the gravel parking area. The trailhead is beside

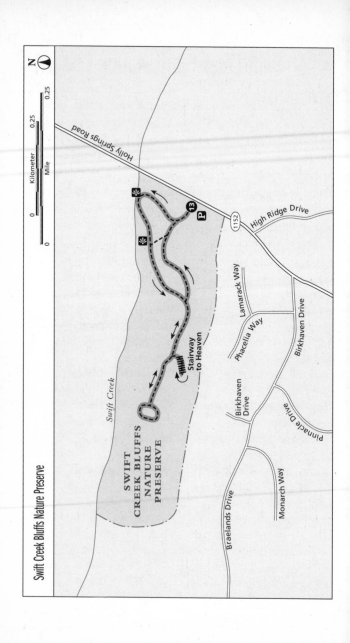

Swift Creek Bluffs Nature Preserve

the kiosk. *DeLorme: North Carolina Atlas & Gazetteer:* Page 40 D1. GPS Coordinates: 35° 43' 03.6" N / 78° 45' 11.7" W

The Hike

Swift Creek Bluffs Nature Preserve offers some of the same sights as Hemlock Bluffs Nature Preserve. Both preserves feature sheer bluffs overlooking Swift Creek that support a mountain-like ecology. Swift Creek Bluffs allows you to experience the landscape in a different way from Hemlock Bluffs, with more rugged trails, including one that passes directly beneath the bluffs.

Unlike much of the region, there are few pine trees here. The forest is mainly hardwood, with bitternut hickory, swamp chestnut oaks, sweet gum, American elm, and river birch.

This small park is a rich bird habitat. Woodpeckers, owls, and hawks make their homes here, as well as many songbirds. The Beech Bluffs Trail is an especially good place for birding, with open canopies below the bluffs.

The large, marked trailhead is right next to the parking lot. Bear right at the first fork to head down toward Swift Creek. The initial part of the hike is through a scrubby forest that is home to critters such as lizards, snakes, rabbits, and raccoons.

As you continue along the creek, there are several access points where you can stop to enjoy the sights. Where the trail branches, stay along the river, eventually making your way under the bluffs. Some very large sweet gum trees grow here. Hollies grow in the sandy soil of the bank and help support the thriving bird population.

From under the bluffs turn back to the previous intersection. This time, ascend the "Stairway to Heaven" to get a view from the top of the bluffs. The stairway is steep but sturdy, and there are benches along the short ascent. More benches at the top invite you to take your time appreciating the view of the river and forest below.

From this point you can continue on your own to the end of the preserve. This is a pleasant hike, but not particularly notable except for connecting to the Birkhaven Greenway Trail.

Make your way back down the stairway to head toward the parking lot. Bear right on the way back to stay on the outside of the loop, and you'll pass through Overcup Oak Swamp, which attracts migratory waterfowl. This section is a flat, easy hike through more mature forests than the riverbank.

Miles and Directions

0.0 Begin at the trailhead beside the kiosk. Soon you will turn right at first intersection to hike along Swift Creek.

0.1 Overlook on the banks of Swift Creek.

0.3 Continue straight at the intersection.

0.4 Continue straight at the intersection, still following the creek.

0.5 Bear right, following the spur trail to Beech Bluff.

0.6 Reach the end of this spur. Enjoy the view of Swift Creek and turn back to the previous intersection.

0.7 At the intersection turn right and ascend the Stairway to Heaven.

0.8 At the top of the stairs is a beautiful view of Swift Creek and a bench where you can rest. Head back down the stairs.

0.9 At the base of the stairs go straight ahead, back toward the parking area.

1.0 Keep right at the intersection. Walk through the Overcup Oak Swamp, a good place to see ducks, salamanders, and turtles. Cross the footbridge and continue straight.

1.2 Continue straight at the intersection. Arrive back at the trailhead.

14　Harris Lake County Park

This hike follows the shore of the Shearon Harris Reservoir for about 3 miles, then veers into the woods for the return leg. The highlight of the hike is a long series of switchbacks following the banks of the reservoir. The continuous elevation change is great for hikers looking for an extra challenge. The final leg of the hike passes the historic Womble Homesite, with marked points of interest.

Distance: 4.2-mile loop
Approximate hiking time: 3–4 hours
Difficulty: Moderate due to some hills
Trail surface: Forested trails
Best seasons: Winter and spring
Other trail users: Joggers, dog walkers
Canine compatibility: Leashed dogs permitted
Fees and permits: No fees or permits required
Schedule: 8:00 a.m.–sunset.

Closed Thanksgiving Day, December 24 and 25, and January 1.
Water availability: Fountain
Maps: USGS Cokesbury, NC; trail map available at trailhead
Jurisdiction: Wake County Parks, Recreation and Open Space (PROS) Department
Trail contacts: Harris Lake County Park, 2112 County Park Drive, New Hill 27562; (919) 387-4342; www.wakegov.com/parks/harrislake/default.htm

Finding the trailhead: From Interstate 40 East take exit 293 (U.S. Highway 64 West/U.S. Highway 1 South). Continue on US 1 South to exit 89 (New Hill). Turn left onto New Hill-Holleman Road. Drive about 3 miles, then turn right onto County Park Drive (at the Harris Lake sign). Follow County Park Drive to the end, parking in the lot nearest the picnic shelters. The trailhead is at the kiosk on your right as you enter the lot. *DeLorme: North Carolina Atlas & Gazetteer:* Page 39 D7. GPS Coordinates: 35° 37' 12.1" N / 78° 55' 38.6" W

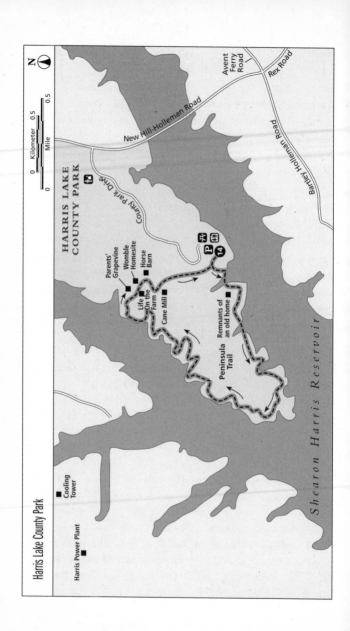

Harris Lake County Park

The Hike

Harris Lake County Park is one of the largest parks in Wake County, covering 680 acres adjacent to Shearon Harris Reservoir. The park was created in cooperation with Progress Energy, which operates the nearby Shearon Harris Nuclear Power Plant. The plant uses the reservoir for cooling, and the 526-foot cooling tower is easily visible from much of the park.

The park features well-maintained gardens, playgrounds, picnic areas, and bathroom facilities. There is also a disc golf course and 7 miles of dedicated mountain bike trails.

The park's major hiking trail, the Peninsula Trail, follows the lakeside for several miles. This begins as a flat, easy stroll, but on the north side of the peninsula, the route begins to switch back and forth to follow the fingers of the lake. This section continues for about 2 miles and should pose a fun challenge for more advanced day hikers.

The final leg of the hike departs from the lake and passes through land once farmed by the Womble family as early as the 1700s. Trail markers indicate features such as the Womble Homesite, a horse barn, and abandoned farm equipment. Most of the woodlands here are well established, with open areas and massive trees. Bird-watching is popular here, with woodpeckers being an especially common resident.

Miles and Directions

0.0 Begin at the trailhead kiosk.

0.1 Turn right onto the small footbridge, then bear left at the fork. At the second fork bear left again, following the sign to the Peninsula Trail.

0.2 Bear left at the next fork.

0.3 Turn left onto the footbridge. Continue straight past the next intersection.

0.7 Continue straight at the intersection.

0.9 Stay on the trail as it begins to run parallel to a service road.

1.0 Informational kiosk.

1.1 Bear left at the fork.

1.5 The trail winds northeast, switching back along the fingers of the lake for the next 2 miles.

3.5 Just after the small footbridge, turn right onto the service road.

3.6 Turn right off the service road into the woods, then bear right onto another service road.

3.7 Continue straight at intersection, passing the historic Womble Homesite on your left.

3.8 Turn left at the intersection.

3.9 At the fork take either leg, rejoining in 0.1 mile.

4.0 Continue straight across service road.

4.1 Bear right at the fork. This will return you to the beginning of the Peninsula Trail.

4.2 Return to the trailhead.

15 Occoneechee Mountain Loop Trail

This rugged loop trail takes you to all four corners of Occoneechee Mountain State Natural Area. The trail begins with a scenic hike winding up and down the mountain, with views of the surrounding forests and pyrophyllite mine. Lovely groves of rhododendron and mountain laurel make this one of the most unique hikes in the area. Next, descend along the base of Occoneechee Mountain and make your way along a shady stretch of the Eno River. An open, sunny woodland stroll brings you back to the parking area. As you scout the varied terrain, be on the lookout for the rare Brown Elfin butterfly, which can be found nowhere else within 100 miles.

Distance: 2.4-mile loop
Approximate hiking time: 1-2 hours
Difficulty: Moderate due to some rocky areas and hills
Trail surface: Forested trail
Best seasons: Spring and fall
Other trail users: Joggers, dog walkers
Canine compatibility: Leashed dogs permitted
Fees and permits: No fees or permits required
Schedule: November–February: 8:00 a.m.–6:00 p.m.; March, April, October, and September: 8:00 a.m.–8:00 p.m.; May–August: 8:00 a.m.–9:00 p.m. Closed December 25.
Water availability: None
Maps: USGS Efland and Hillsborough, NC; trail map available at trailhead
Jurisdiction: NC Division of Parks and Recreation
Trail contacts: Occoneechee Mountain State Natural Area, 6101 Cole Mill Road, Durham 27705; (919) 383-1686; www .ncparks.gov/Visit/parks/ocmo/main.php

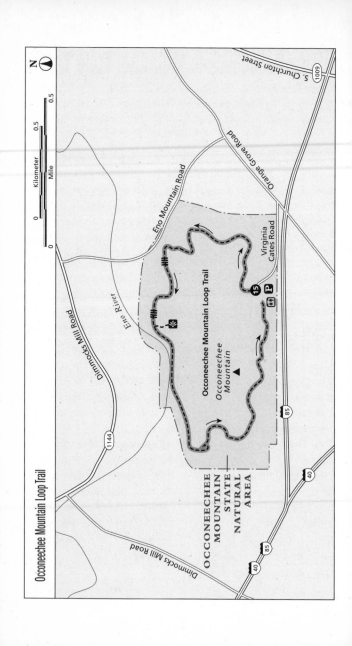

Occoneechee Mountain Loop Trail

Finding the trailhead: From Interstate 85, take the South Churchton Street exit toward Hillsborough. Turn right (north) onto South Churchton Street and travel 0.1 mile. Turn left onto Mayo Street and take it to the end. Turn left onto Orange Grove Road and go about 0.4 mile, then turn right onto Virginia Cates Road (just before the overpass). Follow Virginia Cates Road into the park. From the parking lot, walk to the road and go toward the ranger's residence, then turn right at the trail intersection. There is a kiosk with maps at the trailhead. *DeLorme: North Carolina Atlas & Gazetteer:* Page 39 A5. GPS Coordinates: 36° 03' 41.3" N / 79° 07' 00.1" W

The Hike

Occoneechee Mountain is the highest point in Orange County at 867 feet and the site of a former pyrophyllite mine. Pyrophyllite is found extensively throughout central North Carolina, and a similar mine still operates within sight of the park.

One of the youngest natural areas in the state, the first 124 acres of Occoneechee Mountain State Natural Area were acquired by the state in 1999. In 2006 an additional 66 acres were purchased. Most of the Occoneechee Mountain Loop Trail tours this new land.

The mountain and surrounding lands are mostly forested. Large stands of chestnut oak are found here, as are deer, groundhogs, and wild turkeys. The Brown Elfin butterfly is found here, with no other population known within 100 miles.

Begin your hike from the parking lot. Walk up the service road, turning right at the kiosk just before the ranger's residence. As you emerge into the meadow, bear left back into the forest, following the post.

The first segment of the hike winds uphill. From here

you will have excellent views of the nearby pyrophyllite mine. As the trail levels out, you will enter groves of rhododendron and mountain laurel. This is one of the most charming parts of the hike, with a secluded and mountainous character. Emerge from the switchbacks into a power transmission tower right-of-way. The trail descends steeply downhill here before turning back into the forest.

As the trail descends you will have a good view of the town of Hillsborough. At the bottom the trail passes the base of Occoneechee Mountain. This is the site of the former mine, and in recent years rockslides have left enormous boulders at the base of the cliff. Climbing is not permitted. This is an excellent place for photos and a great place to see vultures, hawks, and other birds of prey.

From the base of the mountain, head down to the Eno River. Note the large galax specimens growing up the bluffs to your left. Follow the river for a short distance before turning back into the woods once more.

The final mile of the hike winds through mixed deciduous/pine forest. Rocks protrude from the ground at times, but the trail is mostly stable and well maintained. The trail emerges on the other side of the parking lot from where you began.

Miles and Directions

0.0 Begin at trailhead.

0.1 Immediately after you emerge into the meadow, turn left into the woods (follow white arrow).

0.4 Go straight at the intersection to stay on the loop trail. To the east (right) there is a beautiful view of another pyrophyllite quarry still active today.

0.7 Another great view of the quarry before the first set of stairs.

1.0 More stairs, then a fork. Keep right to follow the trail.

1.1 The trail meets the Eno River.

1.4 Cross a footbridge, then trail bends left.

2.4 Arrive back at the trailhead.

16 Cox Mountain Trail

Cox Mountain Trail is a challenging uphill climb at the popular Few's Ford access area of Eno River State Park. The trail begins at the Eno River, passing over a swaying suspension bridge. You'll leave the crowds behind as you hike up Cox Mountain Trail. The trail levels out and becomes a relaxing stroll through open mixed deciduous/pine forests before an easy descent to a western section of the river. Take the long way back around Cox Mountain to head back toward the trailhead.

Distance: 2.8-mile loop
Approximate hiking time: 1–2 hours
Difficulty: More challenging due to steep climbs
Trail surface: Forested trail
Best seasons: Spring and fall
Other trail users: Joggers, dog walkers
Canine compatibility: Leashed dogs permitted
Fees and permits: No fees or permits required
Schedule: May–August: 8:00 a.m.–9:00 p.m.; March, April, October, and September: 8:00 a.m.–8:00 p.m.; November–February: 8:00 a.m.–6:00 p.m.
Water availability: Fountain
Maps: USGS Hillsborough, NC; trail map available at trailhead
Jurisdiction: NC Division of Parks and Recreation
Trail contacts: Eno River State Park, 6101 Cole Mill Road, Durham 27705; (919) 383-1686; www.ncparks.gov/Visit/parks/enri/main.php

Finding the trailhead: From Interstate 85 in Durham, take the Cole Mill Road exit. Turn right (north) onto Cole Mill Road and take it to the end. The road will dead-end into the Few's Ford access of the Eno River State Park. Park in the last parking area. The trailhead is in

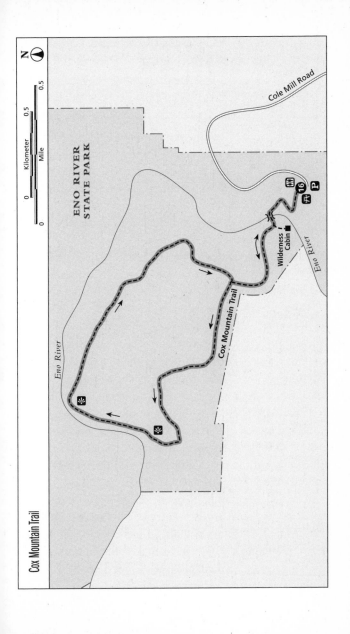

Cox Mountain Trail

ENO RIVER STATE PARK

Eno River

Cox Mountain Trail

Wilderness Cabin

Eno River

Cole Mill Road

N

Kilometer   0.5

Mile   0.5

16   P

front of the handicap parking spaces. *DeLorme: North Carolina Atlas & Gazetteer:* Page 39 A6. GPS Coordinates: 36° 04' 25.9" N / 79° 00' 22.7" W

The Hike

Few's Ford is the largest and most popular of the four Eno River State Park access areas. Three parking lots lead to eight trails covering a total of 12 miles.

The Cox Mountain trailhead is accessible from the second parking lot. The trailhead is large and well marked. Make your way down the switchbacks toward the river, enjoying the view on the way down.

The trail meets the river and briefly follows the bank to a large suspension footbridge. The swaying bridge is a memorable feature of the park. Cross the river here.

Continue straight at the intersection just after the bridge. At this point you will begin to leave the crowds behind as you make your way uphill. At the sign, turn left to begin the loop. You will begin a steep uphill climb. In the next 0.25 mile you will gain over 200 feet of altitude, but there are benches along the trail where you can rest and catch your breath.

When you reach the power transmission towers, you've made it to the highest point of the hike. From here there is a nice view of the surrounding hills, and the hike becomes a gently rolling woodland stroll.

The trail descends more gently than it rose, bringing you down to the westernmost section of the Eno River accessible by trail in the park. This section of the river is very rocky, providing a good habitat for crayfish and other river life. This section of the trail is well traveled and will remain muddy for several days after a good rainfall.

The trail follows the river for about a third of a mile, then veers right. This wooded walk continues for about a mile before you find yourself on a familiar trail, passing the hill where you began the loop.

Miles and Directions

0.0 Begin at the trailhead by the parking lot. Wind your way down toward the river.

0.2 Cross the suspension footbridge over the Eno River.

0.3 Continue straight at the intersection.

0.7 Turn left at the intersection, climbing up a steep section.

0.9 The trail meets the Eno River.

1.2 The trail leaves the river, headed uphill.

2.0 Bear right at two intersections.

2.2 Continue straight, passing the intersection where you began your climb.

2.6 Cross over the suspension footbridge again.

2.8 Back at the parking lot and trailhead.

Clubs and Trail Groups

These local organizations protect, preserve, and advocate for North Carolina's hiking trails and natural areas.

Ellerbe Creek Watershed Association
A nonprofit organization dedicated to protecting, restoring, and enhancing Ellerbe Creek and adjacent land.

Ellerbe Creek Watershed Association
P.O. Box 2679
Durham, NC 27705-2679
(919) 698-8161
contact-us@ellerbecreek.org
www.ellerbecreek.org

The Eno River Association
A nonprofit organization working since 1966 to "conserve and protect the natural, cultural, and historic resources of the Eno River basin."

Eno River Association
4419 Guess Road
Durham, NC 27712
(919) 620-9099
association@enoriver.org
www.enoriver.org

Friends of the Mountains-to-Sea Trail
A nonprofit organization dedicated to the "completion and long-term stewardship" of the Mountains-to-Sea Trail.

Friends of the Mountains-to-Sea Trail
P.O. Box 10431
Raleigh, NC 27605
(919) 698-9024
kdixon@ncmst.org or jdbrewer@bellsouth.net
www.ncmst.org

The Friends of West Point Park
A nonprofit organization "whose purpose is to protect and enhance West Point on the Eno Park."

The Friends of West Point Park
5101 North Roxboro Street
Durham, NC 27704
info@fowpp.org
www.fowpp.org

Land for Tomorrow
A statewide partnership of "concerned citizens, businesses, interest groups, and local governments urging the General Assembly to provide $200 million a year, for five years, to protect the state's land and water resources before they are irreversibly lost."

Land for Tomorrow
4705 University Drive, Suite 290
Durham, NC 27707
(919) 403-8558
info@landfortomorrow.org
www.landfortomorrow.org

The Nature Conservancy – North Carolina Chapter
TNC is a leading conservation organization, founded in 1951. The North Carolina chapter has protected nearly 700,000 acres across the state.

The Nature Conservancy
4705 University Drive, Suite 290
Durham, NC 27707
(919) 403-8558
www.nature.org

North Carolina Birding Trail
A partnership to establish a driving trail linking birding sites across the state. The organization hopes to "conserve and enhance North Carolina's bird habitat by promoting sustainable bird-watching activities, economic opportunities, and conservation education."

NC Wildlife Resources Commission
1722 Mail Service Center
Raleigh, NC 27699-1722
(919) 604-5183
info@ncbirdingtrail.org
www.ncbirdingtrail.org

North Carolina Conservation Network
A "statewide network of over 120 environmental, community, and environmental justice organizations focused on protecting North Carolina's environment and public health. The NC Conservation Network supports, trains, and coordinates diverse groups and directly advocates to achieve equitable and sustainable solutions for our environment."

North Carolina Conservation Network
19 East Martin Street, Suite 300
Raleigh, NC 27601
(919) 857-4699
www.ncconservationnetwork.org

Sierra Club – North Carolina Chapter

The Sierra Club is a leading conservation organization founded in 1892 with the mission "to explore, enjoy, and protect the planet." The North Carolina chapter has operated since 1970 and advocates for environmental causes.

Sierra Club – NC Chapter
112 South Blount Street
Raleigh, NC 27601
(919) 833-8467
northcarolina.sierraclub.org

About the Authors

Peter and Lauren Reylek are avid hikers who live in Durham, North Carolina. In 2006 they launched TrailsofNC .com, an online resource for hiking in North Carolina featuring photographs and detailed trail information.

WHAT'S SO SPECIAL ABOUT UNSPOILED, NATURAL PLACES?

Beauty   Solitude   Wildness   Freedom   Quiet   Adventure

Serenity   Inspiration   Wonder   Excitement

Relaxation   Challenge

There's a lot to love about our treasured public lands, and the reasons are different for each of us. Whatever your reasons are, the national **Leave No Trace** education program will help you discover special outdoor places, enjoy them, and preserve them—today and for those who follow. By practicing and passing along these simple principles, you can help protect the special places you love from being loved to death.

THE PRINCIPLES OF **LEAVE NO TRACE**

- Plan ahead and prepare
- Travel and camp on durable surfaces
- Dispose of waste properly
- Leave what you find
- Minimize campfire impacts
- Respect wildlife
- Be considerate of other visitors

AMERICAN HIKING SOCIETY

Because you hike.
We're with you every step of the way

American Hiking Society gives voice to the more than 75 million Americans who hike and is the only national organization that promotes and protects foot trails, the natural areas that surround them, and the hiking experience. Our work is inspiring and challenging, and is built on three pillars:

Volunteerism and Stewardship

We organize and coordinate nationally recognized programs—including Volunteer Vacations, National Trails Day ®, and the National Trails Fund—that help keep our trails open, safe, and enjoyable.

Policy and Advocacy

We work with Congress and federal agencies to ensure funding for trails, the preservation of natural areas, and the protection of the hiking experience.

Outreach and Education

We expand and support the national constituency of hikers through outreach and education as well as partnerships with other recreation and conservation organizations.

Join us in our efforts. Become an American Hiking Society member today!

American Hiking Society

1422 Fenwick Lane · Silver Spring, MD 20910 · (800) 972-8608
www.AmericanHiking.org · info@AmericanHiking.org